MW01612177

Achievement Equation: Your Formula For Success

Anthony "Tony" R. Reed, CPA, PMP

www.AchievementEquation.com

Other Books by Anthony Reed

Running Shoes Are Cheaper Than Insulin:

Marathon Adventures On All Seven Continents

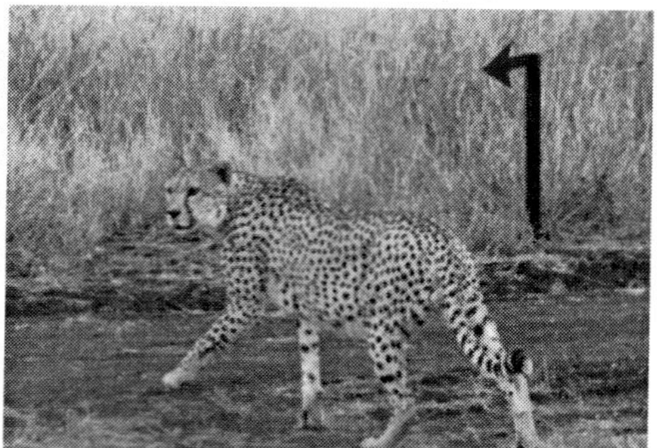

(Yes. That's a cheetah on the course.)

By
Anthony "Tony" Reed, CPA

Dedication

To our children. May they learn from my few successes and my many mistakes.

Acknowledgements

I extend my thanks and appreciation to Deborah Valrie for encouraging me to pursue my dreams and strengthening my faith.

Contact Information

Mr. Reed may be contacted for speaking or consulting engagements at

Anthony Reed, CPA
PO Box 180912
Dallas, TX 75218
214-257-0469
tonyreed@reed-cpa.com
www.AchievementEquation.com

MEMBER
NSA™
NATIONAL SPEAKERS ASSOCIATION

Copyright Notice

Copyright 2007 by Anthony R. Reed, CPA, PMP
All rights reserved.

Without limiting the rights under copyright reserved above, no part of this book may be reproduced, stored in, or introduced into a retrieval system, or transmitted, in any form, or by any means (electronic, photocopying, recording, scanning, uploading, mechanical, reproducing, or otherwise) without the prior written permission of the copyright owner.

ISBN: 978-0-9800215-3-0 (paperback)

Printed in the United States of America

First Printing – September, 2007
Second Printing – September, 2008

Published by Anthony R. Reed, CPA PC

Table of Contents

Achievement

Noun: something accomplished, especially by superior ability, *special effort*, great courage, etc.

Synonyms: Achievement connotes final accomplishment of something noteworthy, after much effort and often *in spite of obstacles and discouragements.*

Source: *Dictionary.com*

Introduction

Over the years, the Achievement Equation has evolved into a powerful tool to meet, if not exceed, your personal and professional goals. The Achievement Equation draws you into the nexus where business strategies and endurance running strategies overlap.

Our process brings into focus those points where project management skills converge with distance running techniques to produce outstanding results. The business strategies include project, change, and time techniques. The running techniques include stress and risk management, pacing, and goal setting.

The Achievement Equation draws from the combined experience of high achieving individuals from around the world. It makes no difference whether the individual manages a quarter billion dollar portfolio or the complicated social dynamics of a small African village, each draws from compatible, if not identical, equations for success.

Successful students, refugee camp managers, professional athletes, runners, bicyclists, ministers, traditional leaders, educators, mountain climbers, and business people, among others, rely on the same variables in the Achievement Equation.

Despite our varied backgrounds, we shared a common characteristic: our ability to overcome failure and obstacles. People are impressed with my academic background; two undergraduate degrees (mathematics and management), an MBA (management), and an MS (accounting). I was also a member of the Accounting Honor Society. Later, I was selected as a Notable Alum by my undergraduate university's alumni association. Also, as an adjunct college professor, I taught accounting, project management, business management, tax, tax, and IT courses. However, in my junior year in college I received a letter, which read, in part:

"*After reviewing your academic records for the past and previous semesters, I have decided that you should be placed on Academic Suspension status.*"

It was from the university's Assistant Dean. I was suspended for poor grades. Not only did I lose my scholarship, but also my residential advisor position.

In order for me to achieve the goal of obtaining a college degree, I had to overcome a major obstacle. Me.

When I overcame that self-imposing obstacle, my academic performance improved. This was followed by decades of success in business, and sports.

The Achievement Equation Components

A job recruiter contacted my three job references to discuss my qualifications for an executive position. Near the end of each phone call, he asked them the same open-ended question, "In three words or less, how would you best describe Tony?" Much to his surprise, they used the same phrase; "goal-oriented."

He then asked them to give one or two specific instances that supported their description. They each gave accounts of situations in completely different areas to support their description. One person focused on my literary, academic, and professional certification achievements. Another emphasized my athletic accomplishments. And the third stressed my professional project management completions.

The recruiter was so impressed that he encouraged me to write a book. Subsequently, I wrote my first book; The SMART Degree – A Young Professional's Guide To Reality. SMART was an acronym for systems, management, accounting, and related technologies. This led to national speaking engagements about multi-disciplinary goal setting.

Over the next few years, I followed up with some of the attendees. I found that their lives had not changed very much. They set the goals, but didn't know how to implement them. This led to frustration and abandonment of their dreams.

As I re-examined my personal life and talked with other achievers, it became obvious that goal setting was just one of four components that are necessary to reach our objectives. The other components were motivation, planning, and execution. Failure to follow through on any one of these components leads to a failure to achieve the goals.

Failure to set goals, leads to a life without direction. This person is aimless. He may be well motivated, but without a goal (or direction), he's like a dog chasing his tail. There's a lot of activity running around in circles. And when you're finished, you're standing right where you started. And you're tired and frustrated.

A lack of motivation means that even the most well defined goal may never be achieved. The individual is too lazy to execute their plan. Or they may start and stop only to never finish. Think about the number of people who say that they want a diploma or degree, but fail to graduate from high school or college.

Once a goal is properly defined and the person is well motivated, they must develop a plan. Without a plan, a person wastes precious energy and resources. The resources include money, other people's time and energy, and materials. Once people see that you're wasting resources, they may not want to help you.

Also, good planning forces you to face the risks associated with reaching your goals. These risks represent your weaknesses. If you don't acknowledge and mitigate your risks/weaknesses before you execute your plan, you may find yourself making the wrong decisions under stress and wasting resources. You must face your weaknesses to succeed.

And last, but not least, failure to execute the plan means that the goal will not be achieved. Many well thought out plans have been left on the floor because people weren't motivated to execute the individual tasks. It's ironic that execute is not only defined as a positive action (to perform), but also as a negative action (to kill). This final component ultimately "makes or breaks" the Achievement Equation.

The Achievement Equation

AE
=
G x M x P x E

Where values G, M, P, and E are binary

The four components are goal setting, motivation, planning, and execution. They work together to form the Achievement Equation.

After realizing the relationship between the components, I found myself accepting and completing more challenging assignments as a business executive. Our vice president of finance called me into his office to discuss a proposal for a global information technology project. We needed to upgrade all the business' mission critical Oracle applications. These included the financial, order management, supply chain, logistics, sales, and web store applications.

He estimated the project would cost between $10 and $12 million. His estimate was based on his research of previous upgrades and the original cost to implement the applications. He wanted me put together a proposal and budget for the project.

A couple of weeks later, I returned with a high level project plan and a proposed budget. I had estimated that the project would cost about $4 million. This was substantially less than his estimate. Needless to say, there was a lot of reservation on his part that the plan would succeed.

About a year later, we discovered that my estimate was incorrect. The project was completed at a cost of $2.6 million!!! It was on time, under budget, and to specifications.

Achievement Equation Component #1

GOAL SETTING

Goal - The result or achievement toward which effort is directed; aim; end.

Source: *Dictionary.com*

The Great Wall of China Marathon Medal

"Far better it is to dare mighty things, to win glorious triumphs, even though check-ered by failure, than to take rank with those poor spirits who nei-ther enjoy much nor suffer much, because they live in the ***<u>gray twilight</u>*** *that knows not victory nor defeat."*

\- Theodore Roosevelt

Bitten by the genealogy bug a decade or so ago I began to collect information on near and distant family members. However, a few years into my research, my system of manila folders—each neatly labeled with a separate branch of the family—had failed to keep pace with the volume and complexity of newly discovered relationships. (My great-grandfather had about twenty-five children.)

As a consequence I invested in a computer software package to map my family tree. Beyond the merits of its relational database the genealogy software yielded unexpected dividends in the form of self-reflection.

Like most people, I offered myself as the ceremonial guinea pig for the first entry and completed the usual fill-in-the-blank fields on the first screen.

- Name
- Place and Date of Birth
- Parents
- Schools Attended
- Last Known Residency

However, the second screen instructed users to write a short story about the family member. For the first time, I found myself asking:

- What do I want people to say about me after I'm dead?
- Which of my accomplishments or achievements will "stand the test of time"?
- Do I want them to say that I was good employee of XYZ Company for 30 years?

"It's pretty hard for the Lord to guide you if you haven't made up your mind which way you want to go."

– Mme. C.J. Walker

Great Wall of China Marathon – Directional Arrow

- Do I want them say that I was the best CPA or project manager?
- What will inspire future generations to overcome obstacles to achieve goals?
- What will live on after I die?

My answers to these and other questions ultimately led me to set and achieve ambitious goals. Goal setting is the first of the four variables of The Achievement Equation. As difficult as this component appears to be, it's the easiest one to complete. You simply state or write your goal.

Like many high school students, my goal was to go to college. And like many students, I completed that goal: I went to college, AND unfortunately, I got kicked out. Surprisingly, this is the goal (i.e. "going to college") of many college dropouts whether they left in academic disgrace, in response to a family or personal crisis, or because economic hardship. As my knowledge and contacts expanded, I refined my goal to *graduate* from college in *five years* AND to *earn* a graduate degree without failing or dropping a course.

Some people in the business world refer to the revised goal as a SMART goal.

Simple & Specific
Measurable
Achievable
Realistic
Timely

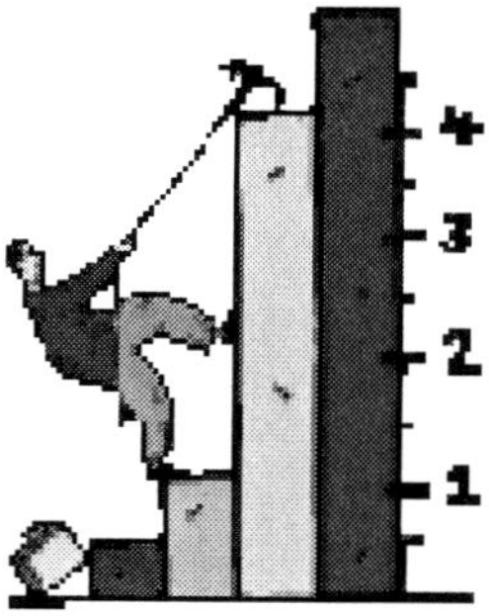

The simple goal of "going to college" failed the SMART test. The goal should have been to *graduate* from college within *five years*. This statement is simple and specific. The revised goal includes a five-year duration. Thus, it's timely.

Based on this timeframe, a student can determine the number of credit hours needed to pass each semester. The operative word here is "*pass*"—contrary to the conventional practice and language of "taking" classes. Thus, for a 120-hour degree program, a student needs to pass 12 credit hours per semester.

This measurement was very realistic. If the student studied hard, turned in assignments on time, asked for assistance when needed, and stopped wasting time, this would be achievable. The combined changes make for a SMART goal.

Organizers of large marathons often erect signs of encouragement along the course. During the Great Wall of China Marathon, we were about to run on one of the more treacherous parts of the course. A sign read, "Arrive in peace, not pieces." This simple sign became the overriding goal for many of my future achievements: to live to set other goals.

Annually, a small number of climbers die while trying to conquer Mt. Everest. Some of them may have felt the moment was their only opportunity. Regardless of the weather, their medical condition, advice from experts, or their climbing experience, they'll put their lives (and, at times, their fellow climbers' lives) at risk

Great Wall of China Marathon Sign

to reach their goal. In "Why Are So Many People Dying on Mt. Everest?" (*British Medical Journal*, August 26, 2006), Dr. Sutherland wrote that once people see the summit, they believe they reach it AND return. Unfortunately, they run out of oxygen.

A few days before the Antarctica Marathon, the runners attended a banquet in Buenos Aires, Argentina. Fate delivered me a seat next to Jeanne Stawiecki. She was attempting to become the first woman in the world to have climbed the highest peak and to run a marathon on all seven continents.

Mt. Everest was her final jewel. She had two previous failed attempts. Her primary goal was not to reach the summit. It was to live. Her second goal was to reach the summit AND return safely. Undeterred, Stawiecki accomplished her goal on May 22, 2007. Our dinner conversation helped me to prioritize my milestone

Definition

Milestone – a significant event in your life or in a project.

Source: *Dictionary.com*

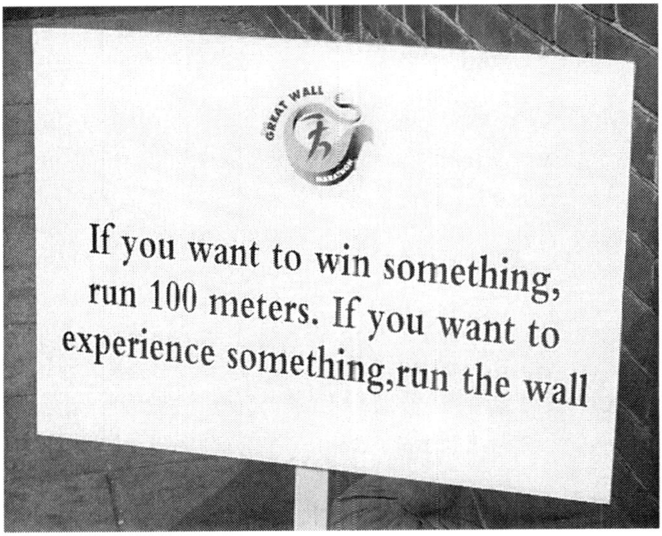

Great Wall of China Marathon Sign

goals for the Antarctica Marathon trip. Milestones are discrete incremental steps on your way to reaching a goal. It's possible to achieve most of your milestones and still miss your main goal.

Several years ago, I trained for a triathlon. It involved swimming, bicycling, and running. Race organizers set the swimming leg at a little over a half-mile in open water. This equated to a one-mile swim in a pool. Thoughts of the swimming portion resurrected a childhood dream to swim a mile.

I spent the summers of my formative years at camps. I progressed through the various swimming certifications. My dream was to be a certified lifeguard. However, I never developed sufficient endurance to swim the mandatory one mile.

The triathlon provided me the opportunity (or excuse) to satisfy my unfulfilled childhood dream of swimming one-mile. By race day, I had achieved the milestone. Unfortunately, events conspired to prevent my finishing the triathlon.

ANTARCTICA MARATHON – THE DRAKE CROSSING & COLLINS GLACIER

Most runners adopted the following milestones for the Antarctica Marathon

1. **Stay alive**. If they failed to finish the race, they could return and try another day.
2. **Set foot on the Antarctica Marathon starting line**. So few people have touched Antarctica, that

just being there was noteworthy.

3. **Finish the half marathon**. Very few people have ever run any race on Antarctica.
4. **Finish the half marathon before the time limit expired**. Once runners met this milestone without any problems, the ultimate goal was within striking distance.
5. **Finish the marathon**.

In the evening, our group departed from Ushuaia, Argentina, on a converted Russian research ship named the R.V. Akademik Ioffe. We headed across the Drake Passage to King George Island, Antarctica. It was one thing to read about the Drake Passage's rough seas in a geography book; it was a completely different thing to experience it firsthand.

The 380-foot ship carries about 160 people, including the staff and crew. By comparison, the Disney cruise line ships are over 900 feet long and carry a couple of thousand people!

The accommodations, staff, and crew were great. The ship's crew informed us that we would either experience "the Drake Lake" (i.e. smooth waters) or "the Drake Quake" (i.e. rough seas). At breakfast the first morning, most of the passengers and the crew were sporting their motion sickness patches. I felt comfort in the notion of being one of many suffering that morning.

For this reason, I considered it an achievement just to be well enough to get to the starting line without suffering from seasickness, having any negative side-

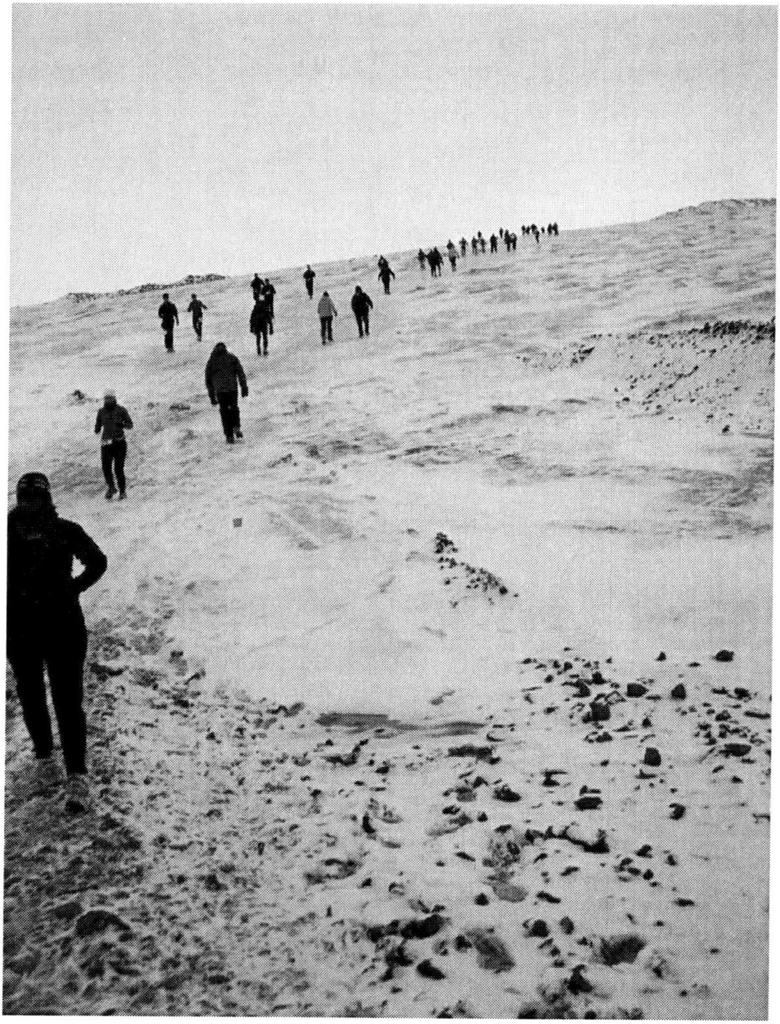

Antarctica Marathon's Collins Glacier

effects from the motion sickness patch, and being able to keep down my food to have energy for the marathon.

Four times during the race, we had to navigate our way through 600 feet of ankle deep mud. Around the 3rd and 17th miles, runners encountered Collins Glacier, a sheet of ice at a 17-degree angle. (Most treadmills only go up to 12 degrees.) We had to run up three-quarters of a mile and run back down. If you slipped on the glacier, there was nothing to grab onto—except another runner.

Since I live and train in Dallas' mild winters and flat terrain, running up and down glaciers in sub-freezing temperatures, blinding snow, and strong winds was going to be a challenge.

Unlike the big city marathons, there were no buildings to shield you from the winds. You were completely at the mercy of Mother Nature. There was absolutely no place to hide.

Also absent from the bleak icescape were the cheering crowds along the race route. Your cheerleaders were your fellow runners, plus the penguins, fur seals, and skua birds. Occasionally, someone from the Russian, Chinese, or Uruguayan research stations would step outside to wave.

After the initial shock and awe of seeing Collins Glacier, it posed a physical challenge for both the ascent and descent. There were no real reference points, such as the end of a street block or building, to visualize progress, just non-stop snow and ice.

The 17-mile approach to the Collins Glacier challenges one's mental resolve. The endless landscape of ice and snow combine with physical exhaustion in ways that break down a runner's mental state. This often results in a runner withdrawing prematurely from the race somewhat disoriented and dangerously exposed to the frigid cold as their body temperature drops from lack of vigorous movement.

Consequently I adopted "keep moving" as my mantra. Stopping would have been hazardous to my health. Thus, the milestone of "keep moving" was directly related to my primary goal of staying alive. I completed the half marathon a full 20 minutes before the cut off time and successfully finished the marathon.

Eight days later, I also completed the Fin Del Mundo Marathon in Ushuaia, Argentina. Unforgettable!

Business projects fail primarily due to unrealistic scope (i.e. goals, milestones), timelines, and resources. Your team risks spiraling into an abyss where living another day is secondary to completing the project.

The project deadline minefield is littered with dead hearts (heart attacks), dead marriages (divorces), dead bodies (death), and dead working relationships (disgruntled staff members). If a project's scope is SMART and properly managed, your deadline will become party time.

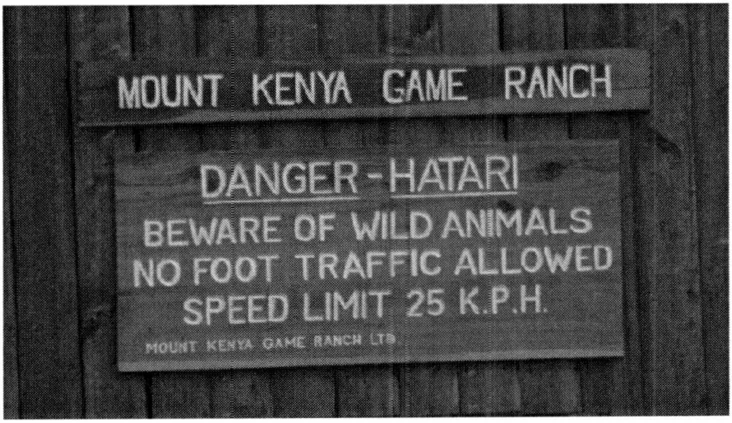

This sign "greeted" us as we prepared to leave the Mount Kenya Game Ranch for a training run. The guard counted the runners as we left and returned. Fortunately, the two numbers were the same.

Great Wall of China Marathon Sign

YOUR BALANCED SCORECARD

One of the problems associated with achieving goals is that we can become too focused in one area and our life becomes disarray. We begin neglecting other aspects of our life. This can lead to a breakdown of our family structure, social circles, health, and faith. Thus, it's important to set goals in five areas.

1. **Mental Goal** – Stay mentally stimulated and alert. Challenge yourself to become a student every few years. Earn an additional degree or certification. Consider becoming a part-time, adjunct professor. Teaching forces you to learn new material well enough to teach it and answer questions. You may decide to read a book a month or complete your newspaper's daily crossword puzzle.

2. **Physical Goal** – A man was once so happy and relieved that he'd reached his goal, that he had a heart attack. The stronger you are physically, the more you can achieve. A person might have a goal of running 100 miles a month. While this may seem like a lot to non-runner, this translates to about 30 minutes a day. Let's face it, most people waste more than 30 minutes a day. Also, the more physically fit you are, the more you will enjoy your retirement.

3. **Social Goal** – Schedule time with your family and friends. One of our goals was to have a family game night on Fridays. Some adopt a personal goal of never missing an event in which their children participated. Plan a weekly "date" night with your spouse. If you don't have your family's support, it may be

difficult and/or costly (divorce) to achieve your goal.

4. **Financial Goal** – Money funds many goals and eases stress. The more money you have, the more goals you can achieve. Thus, it's important to set financial goals. Since you can't get a loan for your retirement, you should be saving for this event, while maintaining a high credit score. Financial problems kill most goals. While money may not buy happiness, you can always use it to wipe away the tears.

5. **Spiritual Goal** – This is the foundation of many people's lives and the biggest stress reliever. You may decide to attend your church, synagogue, temple, or mosque weekly. You may decide to read a daily devotional or prayer. Others may decide to simply spend 30 minutes of "me time" or "quiet time" to re-connect with your inner self.

PUBLIC BROADCAST OR PRIVATE SECRET

Once you've established your SMART goals, you have to decide whether or not to tell people. While in college, I was employed as a computer printer operator. I worked the graveyard shift; 11pm to 8am.

During the month ends, things were always busy. It wasn't unusual for me to be printing for eight hours straight. However, during the rest of the month, things were relatively slow. Many of the computer operators spent their time playing cards and reading comic books or other magazines. I spent my time studying calculus. My co-workers stopped talking with me and started complaining about my work. The next thing I knew, I was fired.

"They smile in your face.
All the time they want to take your place.
The backstabbers."

The Backstabbers, performed by The O'Jays.

A few months later, I was working as a computer programmer. Everything was fine. I went through my probationary period without any problems. I spent my lunch time studying at my desk. One day, a co-worker told me that others were complaining that I wasn't "pulling my weight." They reasoned that if I had time to go to school in the evenings, then I had too much time on my hands.

I decided to start complaining about school and announced my decision to drop out. My co-workers' complaints stopped. I learned that the real problem wasn't with the quantity or quality of my work. My co-workers, many of whom lacked a degree, were surviving. They didn't want to see me thrive. They were threatened by my ambition to succeed in an area where they had failed.

So, several times a week, I quickly ate lunch with my co-workers and then excused myself. I'd go to my car and study. I never mentioned my academic goal again, until my graduation announcement was posted on the bulletin board. A few weeks later, I had resigned and became a fulltime graduate student.

You must decide whether or not to tell others about your goals. You may find yourself surrounded by backstabbers instead of supporters. I realized that it's best to keep some goals to myself until they've been achieved. And be prepared for any backlash by your non-supporters.

Achievement Equation Component #2

MOTIVATION

Motivation

Definition: inducement; incentive.

Motivate

Definition: to incite; impel; induce, move, provoke, prompt, cause.

Source: *Dictionary.com*

HOW MOTIVATION BECAME A PART OF THE EQUATION

Some of us are "pre-programmed" to set goals. A failing high school student will tell you that their goal is to graduate from college. Yet, they're not motivated to study for their high school classes. An adult will tell you that they want a professional certification, such as a CPA. Yet, they won't make the time to study. Articulating the SMART goal was easy. However, they weren't motivated to overcome the obstacles.

Self-motivation was essential for surviving and finishing the Antarctica Marathon. Unlike the televised marathons, such as the New York City Marathon, where you have over 35,000 runners with millions of screaming and supportive spectators, we had about 25 spectators and 200 runners.

Also, we faced obstacles unlike anything we had ever experienced, such as running up glaciers or being chased by fur seals. We also faced obstacles just getting to the race's starting line; crossing the Drake Passage. Thus, if you had low self-motivation or were unprepared for the obstacles, you would quit the race.

You had to be your own cheerleader and inspirational coach. Your mind had to tell your body to keep moving while your body was screaming at you to stop. Self-motivation propels you over the obstacles. It's important to surround yourself with self-motivated people. Self-motivation is infectious. A passenger on the trip was a smoker and a non-runner. He remarked that being in a room full of marathoners was like being

"Unless we start to believe in ourselves, we will never convince anyone to believe in us. It is time to believe in ourselves."

- Ronald H. Brown

at a revival. However, there wasn't an evangelist motivating the crowd. We were very unassuming and yet, highly motivated. He could feel the high energy level in the room. He decided to quit smoking and to start running.

WEAPONS & MOTIVATIONAL SONGS

My karate teacher disliked teaching weapons for self-defense. He felt that the weapons could become your crutch. If you found yourself in a street fight, the chances were great that your weapons were at home. Thus, he emphasized using equipment that you carry with you at all times: your body.

This same logic should apply to self-motivation. You should not depend on other people, such as family, friends, motivational speakers, posters, or props, like portable music players, to motivate you. The best motivator is your memories. They're always with you.

I've seen runners have emotional breakdowns during marathons because their MP3 died. The battery ran out of juice. The player got wet. It got damaged during a fall. The player contained their catalog of 150 motivational songs. Now, for the first time in their months of training, their motivator was gone.

It's better to memorize the motivational songs than to rely on a portable player. If you forget the words to the song, you can have fun making up your own version!!!

"Lord, make me so un-comfortable that I do the very thing I fear."

- Ruby Dee

SELF-MOTIVATION FOUNDATION

I believe that motivation is based more on fear rather than love. Even when motivation is driven by love, it may actually be the fear of losing the loved one that causes us to take action. Fear of poverty and homelessness drives me go to work, not the love of my job. Fear of freezing to death drove me to keep moving during the Antarctica Marathon, not the love of running.

LONG JUMP CRISIS

In high school, I was a long jumper. Initially, my longest jump was around 15 feet. At a track meet, I was shocked as I stared down a rival high school's long jump runway. My high school's take off board was about 3 feet from our long sand pit. This board was about 16 feet from the short sand pit!!!

I watched in horror as a fellow jumper sprinted down the runway, took off from the board, came up short, landed very hard on the runway surface, and tumbled into the sand pit. I was too scared to take a practice jump. All I could think about injuring myself and coming up with an excuse for not jumping.

When my name was called, I was still scared. I ran down the runway, took off, extended myself in mid air, and blacked out. Much to my surprise, I landed in the pit. I had obviously fouled by taking a step over the board. However, I turned around and saw a white flag waving. It was a fair jump!!!

It measured over 18 feet. From that day forward, I consistently jumped over 18 feet. Fear of hitting the runway inspired me to dramatically improve that day, not the love of long jumping.

FACING FEARS

FEARS is an acronym for a

Failure to
Evaluate
All
Reasonable
Solutions

When faced with an obstacle, I try to identify numerous solutions. The more solutions that I identify, the more comfortable I feel.

Cold fingers were my major concern at the Antarctica Marathon. My fears were mitigated after researching different gloves and mittens. I tried ones made with special materials. Battery-powered, chemically warmed, and "breath" warmed ones were tested. Combinations of wearing gloves in mittens with mitten covers were examined. My fear didn't go away until the problem was resolved.

"In every crisis, there is a message. Crises are nature's way of forcing change – breaking down old structures, shaking loose negative habits so that something new and better can take their place."

\- Susan L. Taylor

THE GREAT WALL OF CHINA MARATHON'S 3,600 STEPS OF FEAR

A couple of days before the Great Wall of China Marathon, we were required to take a walking tour over part of the course. It was the 3-mile section that was actually on The Great Wall. The marathoners ran over this section twice starting around miles 3 and 20.

The Wall was built to go over the steepest hills with the steepest drop offs. After all, it's much harder to attack The Wall while running up a steep hill. Thus, running on The Wall was very challenging.

We started the tour on the rebuilt section. The marathoners had to go up and down about 3,600 steps. This was unlike running on football stadium steps. These steps weren't the same height. Thus, it was very difficult to establish a rhythm. The Wall was not built to OSHA standards!!!

I told myself that I could live with these mild inconveniences. After all, if this were meant to be an easy race, they would not have referred to it as an "adventure" marathon. After about a mile on the rebuilt section, we came to one of the original sections of The Wall. It was here that my initial excitement soon turned to horror.

The Wall's path was about five-feet wide. Since there weren't any handrails, we didn't have much to grab, other than another person, in case we fell. There was a short wall on one side and nothing to prevent us from falling off of the other side. The 50-foot drop offs

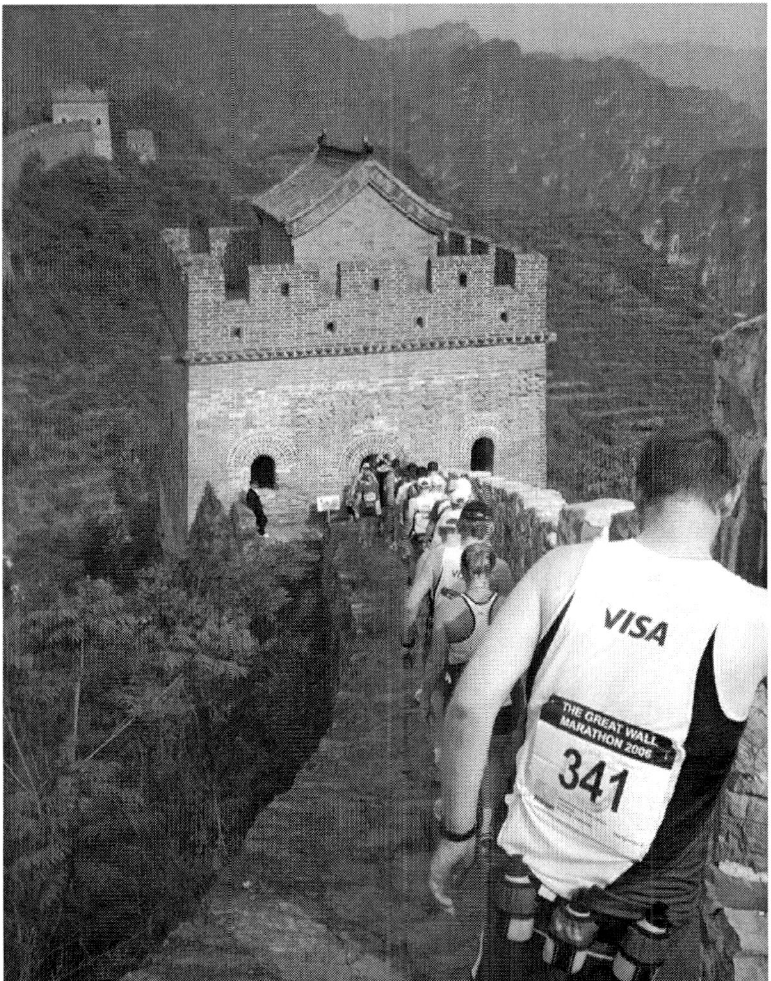

Great Wall of China Marathon

could easily kill us. The rocks were crumbling and smooth. If it rained, we could easily slip and fall. Unfortunately, as the runners were lining up to slowly walk across this section, I was right in front of a chattering adolescent. She asked her parents every question that I didn't want to hear.

- Has anyone died from falling off The Wall?
- How far is that drop?
- Is that far enough to kill you?
- How will they get your body? With a helicopter?
- Will it rain on Saturday?
- How slippery will these rocks get if it rains?
- Will they cancel the race?
- What do you grab to stop you from falling?
- Do you think you could grab a tree limb to keep from falling?
- Is it too late to turn around and go back?

I was very deep in thought on the bus ride back to our hotel. I was scared. I finally decided that I didn't come this far to back out. A race or life without risk is not an adventure. Or as the sign along the course read, "A race without hills is like coffee without caffeine." This was going to be a real adventure.

The only way for me to survive the race was to face my fears and to develop an action plan. I decided to take a lesson from drivers' education. During the treacherous sections of The Wall I would not focus on the people who were behind me. I would not let them influence or pressure me to go faster. I would go at my own, comfortable pace.

I would also maintain a five-foot gap or "safety zone" with the person in front of me. If they fell, they couldn't take me down with them.

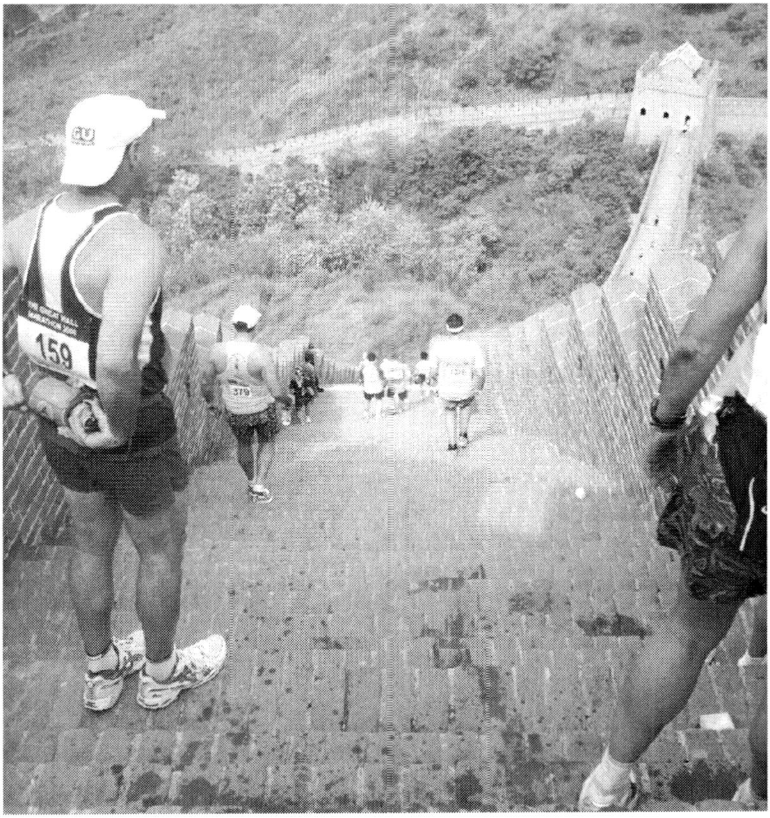

Great Wall of China Marathon

I broke up The Wall into smaller, more manageable tasks. The roomy guard towers became my focal points and rest stops. The faster runners would pass me in the towers.

Also, since hydration was critical, I would drink water while in the towers. If I became dehydrated, I might lose my focus and slip on the stairs. The views from the towers allowed me to savor my past success and look forward to my next adventure.

I wouldn't care about my finishing time. However, the marathon had an eight-hour time limit. This was manageable. My mission was to run a marathon on every continent. It was not to finish the marathons by a certain time or to die in the process. Thus, sanity and risk mitigation prevailed in my planning.

After about seven and a half hours, I crossed the finish line. This was my slowest marathon by almost two hours. However, I didn't care. The Wall was conquered. Later that night, I was looking at the 100 photos from the marathon. It occurred to me that I stopped running for about 60 to 90 seconds to take each photo!!!

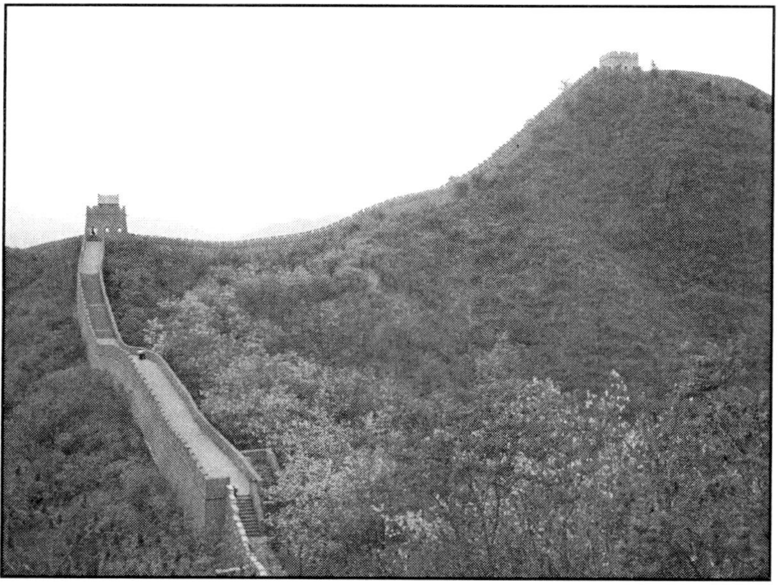

Comfort Zone

Definition: An environment or situation in which a person feels secure or at ease; also figuratively, an established lifestyle in which a person feels comfortable *as long as there is no drastic change*.

Source: *Dictionary.com*

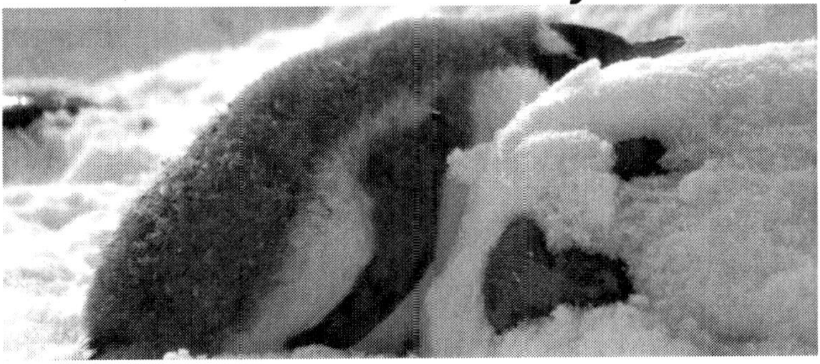

FEARS

Failure to
Evaluate
All
Reasonable
Solutions

The Antarctica Marathon Medal

THE COMFORT ZONE

Right now, you're probably in your comfort zone. There must be a drastic change or challenge to move you from it. The question that you have to answer is: "What role or responsibility do you want to have in managing the change?" In other words, do you want people to force you to drastically change? Or, do you want to plan, control, and implement this drastic change yourself?

To paraphrase Dr. King (p. 42), the only way for you to grow is to accept challenges and move out of your comfort zone.

All of us have comfort zones. There's nothing wrong with having one. Some people have very small comfort zones. For example, I had a relative who was practically born and raised in the same house. She raised her children, and ultimately, retired there. She never learned to drive and rarely left her hometown. She was very content in her very small comfort zone.

However, the wider your comfort zone, the more you can experience and achieve. You simply have more space to work in. You tend to show less fear and more curiosity. In order to widen your zone, you must move outside of it and establish a new outer boundary.

This move may cause stress and pain and also expose your weaknesses. You must face your weaknesses and flaws and develop plans to address them via the FEARS acronym.

"The ultimate measure of a man is not where he stands in moments of comfort and convenience, but where he stands at the time of challenge and controversy."

Dr. Martin Luther King, Jr.

CPA TEST-TAKING CRISIS

After ten years of being out of college, I returned to pursue an accounting master's degree in the evenings. I was the oldest person in most of my classes. As an information technology manager, I was clearly outside of my comfort zone.

Many people had said that information technology professionals didn't understand accounting. Furthermore, I didn't have any role models. If anything, IT and accounting professionals were more adversaries than friends. During my studies, I maintained a very high GPA and was accepted into the National Accounting Honor Society.

After graduation, I began preparing for the 3.5-day Certified Public Accounting (CPA) exam. The exam's four parts were audit, law, practice, and theory. At least 75% on all four parts was required to pass. I had to pass at least two parts during one testing session to receive any credit.

Also, a grade over 50% was required on the parts that I failed. I could retake the failed parts at a later date. Thus, if I received 100% on three parts and 49% on the fourth part, I received no credit and had to retake all four parts!!!

I took a practice CPA exam and received less than 25% on all of the parts. I was devastated. I studied even harder, took another practice exam, and didn't improve. If I wanted to pass, I had to re-examine and revise my studying and test-taking strategies and techniques.

"Decide that you want it more than you're afraid of it."

- Bill Cosby

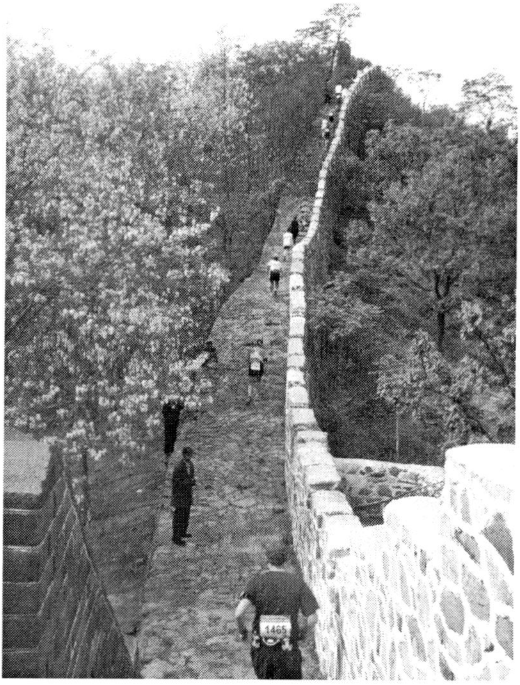

Great Wall of China Marathon

First, I realized that I was repeatedly studying the same topics. These were my favorites and I thoroughly understood them. They represented my comfort zone. However, based on the test results, my favorites only accounted for about 25% of the test. Since there were five options for each question, I was doing slightly better than guessing chances of 20%.

I needed to move out of my comfort zone and study my least favorite topics: income taxes, consolidations and eliminations, and pension accounting, to name a few. This was the only way for me to pass.

Unfortunately, most of us have a habit of focusing on our strengths and avoiding our weaknesses. In order to get ahead, we must move outside of our comfort zones. I forced myself to become as comfortable and proficient with my least favorite topics as my favorite ones. I actually forced myself to stop reverting back to studying my favorite topics.

My next problem was test taking. I hate taking multiple-choice tests. They have an impersonal way of telling me what I don't know—and like most people; I want to feel that I know everything. The CPA exam had hundreds of five-part multiple-choice questions.

I had to overcome my test taking fear and anxiety. I decided to approach each of the five choices as five individual true/false questions. I also forced myself to breathe between each question. This prevented me from unconsciously holding my breath during a stressful situation and losing focus. It's hard to concentrate if your brain is short on oxygen.

I received my CPA license thanks to acknowledging my weaknesses and anxieties and developing plans to overcome them: FEARS. Several years later, I found myself teaching all of my pre-CPA problem areas in collegiate accounting classes. I had to employ this same studying and test-taking strategies while preparing for the Project Management Professional certification.

OTHER PEOPLE'S COMFORT ZONES FOR YOU

Some people don't want to move outside of their personal comfort zones. In some cases, other people don't want you move outside of the comfort zone that THEY'VE established for YOU. They've put you in a box. How many of your co-workers, friends, or relatives have told you that you couldn't do something?

When you achieved the unexpected, it forced them to re-evaluate their perceptions (or prejudices). Think about it. When you did the unexpected, the strongest naysayers felt uncomfortable. It may have shaken their fundamental beliefs about people like you.

After getting suspended, my efforts were refocused on getting back into college and graduating. Once back into college, my GPA had dramatically improved. My senior advisor asked me about my post-graduation plans. I told her that I wanted an MBA.

She looked at me and said that she didn't think that I was "grad school material" and probably won't get admitted. I was shocked to hear this from a person who was supposed to be supportive of my goals.

"It is impossible for a people to rise above their aspirations. If we think we cannot, we almost certainly cannot. Our greatest enemy is our defeatist attitude."

– Robert Williams

Gold Coast (Australia) Airport Marathon Medal

I calmly explained that I had been offered academic scholarships and graduate teaching assistantships from two of the top MBA programs. I was also accepted into a Ph.D. program in mathematics. My advisor promptly walked out.

She had very low expectations of me. Her comfort zone for me was a very small comfort zone. She also felt uncomfortable that I had challenged her perceptions. Her comfort zones for me didn't prevent me achieving academic successes. Subsequently, I earned two graduate degrees and three highly sought after professional certifications; a certificate as a Project Management Professional, Supply Chain Manager, and Certified Public Accountant (CPA).

THE "OPPOSITE" MIND TRAP

Part of moving out of your comfort zone involves changing your mindset. We may start with something as simple our understanding of opposites. We're taught to believe that that you're either a scholar or an athlete; a technical person or a business person; left handed or right handed. This mindset has forced some people to believe that they can't cross over the barrier to the opposite side without a great many sacrifices.

However, when we step back and look at the big picture, we see that opposites are really the same thing and they must co-exist. One cannot exist without the other. For example, you can't have an "off" without its related "on." Think about what happened when someone thought out of the box. They invented the variable dimmer switch. The dimmer focuses on the amount of lightness (or darkness) in small increments. A traditional light switch focuses on the extremes.

This old mindset has prevented athletes from becoming scholars and, conversely, scholars from becoming athletes. When many people see my academic credentials (four degrees), they see a nerd or geek. They visualize an uncoordinated, thick eye-glass wearing, unfit individual. This represents their comfort zone.

They become overwhelmed when they learn about my athletic accomplishments.

- Earned high school letters in track and soccer
- Completed a 100-mile bicycle race
- Completed over ninety 26.2-mile marathons, including winning awards for placing
- Completed marathons on all seven continents, including Antarctica
- Earned a brown belt in karate

I have refused to limit my goals based on other people's low expectations and perceptions. Over the years, I've talked with parents who have seen their smart and bright junior and high students "dummy down" to be with their peers.

Their peers felt that you couldn't be a rap artist, have boyfriends, or be an athlete while being intelligent. Yet, these intelligent people (i.e. doctors, lawyers, accountants, etc.) are the very ones that they'll rely on when they graduate from high school.

Great Wall of China Marathon Sign

Some other deterrents to self-motivation are the various career and success indicators. These are the tests that students take that help determine what career they should pursue. The counterparts, in the business world, are the tests that supposedly predict your success as a manager or executive.

If you truly believe you can be successful in a different field, you should pursue it. Rather than to accept the results of the test as final, think of them as identifying possible weaknesses for you to improve upon.

For example, a career test revealed that I should be in a highly analytical field, such as math or engineering. My math grades also supported the test results. However, I enjoyed sports, writing, public speaking, and art—the "soft" skills.

"Too many people are afraid to look deep down and see where they made mistakes. You have to take an honest look and have an honest evaluation of your performance."

– Tiger Woods
USA Today, March 26, 2007

My professional positions were in the highly analytical fields of computers and accounting. However, I worked equally hard on improving my "soft" skills. I took classes and associated with professionals in those areas.

Subsequently, I became a successful athlete, magazine writer, professional speaker, and photographer. I also served on the board of director for a professional theatrical organization and co-founded a national running organization. All the while, I was still highly analytical.

"I TRIED" TROPHY

I took five steps forward down the hallway. The hallway was outside of the restrooms. During those steps, I pushed the ball out, swung it back, swung it forward, released it, and followed through. All these actions were done with complete control and consistency. This was how Mr. Chisom taught me to bowl at the Ringside Bowl Lanes in St. Louis, Missouri.

I was about six years old and could barely lift the ball, let alone control it. It was a real struggle. When I was on the actual bowling lanes, I was the Gutter Ball King. Despite my lack of talent (and score), every Saturday morning my brother and I showed up.

At the end of the season, they awarded me the first ever "I Tried" trophy. My average was 63. Regardless of the number of gutter balls I had thrown, I never gave up. By the time I was a teenager, I had made it to the finals of the citywide youth bowling tournament.

The funny thing about bowling is that you have to be consistent on your first ball. All ten pins are standing in fixed locations. You usually stand in the same place each time and repeat the same motion for the strike.

However, you have a great deal of flexibility on your second ball to pick up the spare. You change your starting location depending on the pin arrangement. I thrived in this structured, yet flexible environment of bowling.

Today, I find myself reliving and recapturing this "I Tried" spirit. The more gutters I threw, the closer I would get to a strike. It didn't matter how many times I failed. I kept forging ahead with that childlike, "I'll master this thing" mentality. I'd study my mistakes, make an adjustment, and try again.

I've seen this same drive with children trying to master making free throws. They'll stay up past daylight to shoot baskets outside well into the night. I sometimes wonder if as adults, we've developed a "can't do" attitude. This keeps us from trying after a few failures, while children just simply don't know when to stop.

Take a few minutes and think about your fondest childhood memory of overcoming an obstacle. It may have been learning to ride a bicycle, swimming the length of a pool, or running a non-stop lap around a track. Try to recapture that feeling to motivate you as you execute your plan.

Achievement Equation Component #3

PLANNING

Plan

Definition: *Noun:* a scheme or method of acting, doing, proceeding, making, etc., *developed in advance.*

Planning

Definition: *Verb:* to arrange a method or scheme *befo-rehand* for (any work, enter-prise, or proceeding)

Source: *Dictionary.com*

"People don't plan to fail. They fail to plan."

- Unknown

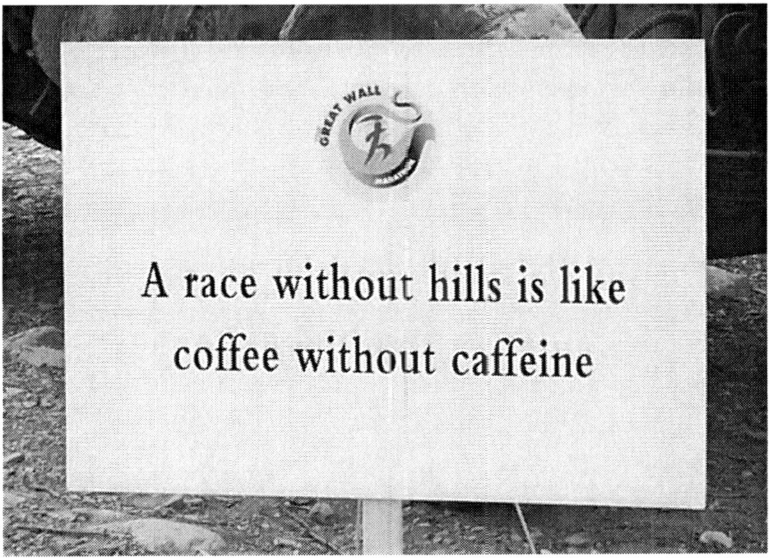

Great Wall of China Marathon Sign

HOW PLANNING BECAME A PART OF THE EQUATION

I've planned and managed projects for almost 30 years. Eventually, I earned my Project Management Professional (PMP) certification. As I talked with highly successful people, I noticed that they were planners. It didn't matter if they were climbing Mt. Everest, running a marathon, leading troops into battle, or heading a global, multi-million dollar company. They were all great planners and it was almost second-nature to them.

Events just didn't "happen." They were well thought out in advance. They successfully translated their SMART goal (or vision) into a project plan. And they motivated people to follow the plan. A good plan consists of more than writing the tasks. You must identify the:

- dependencies between the tasks
- estimated durations
- tasks' start and finish dates, and
- resources used to complete the tasks.

The resources are people, money, or materials. If you have small children, a babysitter might be one of your resources. Most plans fail because something was missing, such as a task or resource. It's important for someone who has achieved the goal, to review your plan for thoroughness. Achievers enjoy helping others by sharing their experiences with novices.

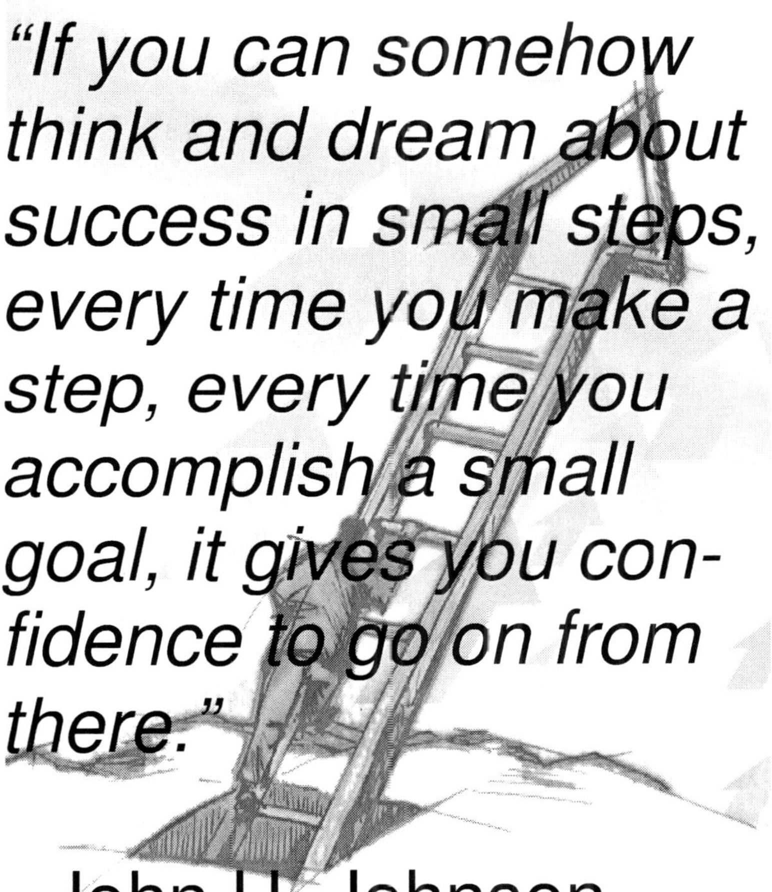

"If you can somehow think and dream about success in small steps, every time you make a step, every time you accomplish a small goal, it gives you confidence to go on from there."

- John H. Johnson

PLANNING PROBLEMS

Three major problems associated with planning are

1. **Failure to manage risks** – Bad things can happen with any plan. We can run out of money. A major resource won't be available. We made need more resources than originally thought. These are things that we may have been aware of during the planning stage, but didn't include in the plan.
2. **Analysis paralysis** – We spend so much time planning, that we never execute the plan. This is almost the opposite of failure to plan for risks. This is the "never ending" planning cycle.
3. **Failure to gain support** – As your plan is executed, you may find that your resources aren't helping you. Furthermore, they don't understand why you're angry with them.

We'll examine each of these problems more closely.

MANAGING RISK

A Mt. Everest climber said, "The person with the most recovery plans wins." This logic is supported by good project planning. When some people develop plans, they assume that everything will go smoothly. However, reality tells us that this isn't always the case. Our failure to recognize and address the potential trouble spots can be very costly.

When contingency plans are constructed for potential problems, the probability for success increases. In

Definitions

Risk - exposure to the chance of injury or loss; a hazard or dangerous chance

Mitigation - to lessen in force or intensity, as wrath, grief, harshness, or pain; moderate.; to make less severe

Recovery - restoration or return to any former and better state or condition.

Source: *Dictionary.com*

"The guy who takes a chance, who walks the line between the known and unknown, who is unafraid of fail-ure, will succeed."

- Gordon Parks

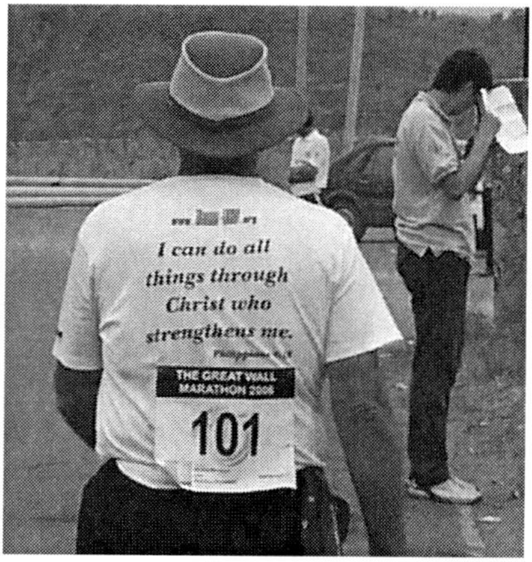

Great Wall of China Marathoner

project planning, this is referred to as risk mitigation and management. You identify the:

- potential problem or risk
- probability of the event occurring
- events that may forewarn that the problem is about to occur
- cost of correcting the problem, if it occurs
- corrective action you plan to take
- individual responsible for monitoring the problem and implementing the corrective action

A good contingency plan reduces the anxiety of dealing with unwanted changes.

MISSING WORKER

After developing the plan for a large multi-million dollar, international project, we asked, "Based on the past projects, what are your concerns?" People leaving before the project's completion was their biggest concern. They could have a:

- major medical problem, such as a heart attack
- better job offer from another company
- get hit by a train
- retire

We couldn't guarantee that none of these events would occur. However, we tried to ensure that all the tasks were in the plan, resources were assigned to the tasks, all of the critical tasks were well documented, and everyone had a backup person who could step in, if needed.

"Mistakes are a fact of life. It is the response to the error that counts."

- Nikki Giovanni

Lewa Safaricom Marathon Medal

A couple of weeks before the implementation date, a key team member went missing. A couple of days passed before his wife called. He was being held in a deportation facility. Needless to say, he wasn't returning to the office.

Our VP ran into my office about the unplanned departure. He thought that the project would certainly fail or be delayed. I explained we had executed the "AWOL" contingency plan. We replaced his name in our plan with that of his pre-assigned backup. Our deadline was unchanged. The project was implemented on time, under budget, and to specifications.

SAFARICOM LEWA MARATHON – RUNNING WITH THE CHEETAHS

Before Kenya's Safaricom Lewa Marathon, we went on photo safaris. It gave us opportunities to see the course. The marathon was held in the Lewa Wildlife Conservancy. We ran twice around a 13.1-mile loop.

As we drove along the dirt road, we were surrounded by fields of tall grasses and mountains, instead of parking lots and buildings. This also meant that were would be almost no cheering crowds and very little shade to block the sun. As it turned out, these were the least of my worries. The animals would be roaming freely during the race!!!

As we rode over a hill, we spotted a couple of rhinos. Our driver and guide told us about the rhino's weight, speed, and temper. We quickly determined that they could outrun us.

We asked the obvious questions.

Q1. What should we do if we encounter a rhino during the marathon?
A1. Stand still and slowly walk backwards.

Q2. What should we do if a rhino charges us?
A2. Zigzag. They're terrible at turning corners.

I made a mental note to conserve my energy in case I had to run sprints. I just hoped that I would be sprinting towards the finish line instead of away from it. At least rhinos aren't predators—which was one good thing at least. They don't hunt and eat people. That was a big relief.

Over the next hill, we spotted three cheetahs. They were walking on the course and looking at the course directional signs. This was a little nerve racking. The guide explained that the cheetahs may be brothers. They were very strong and fast, hunt as a single unit, and can quickly bring down a zebra.

As we watched the cheetahs locking at the course and looking back at us, we felt that it wasn't worth asking the same questions about the cheetahs that we'd asked about the rhinos. Once a cheetah looked at us on the course, we felt that we couldn't outrun it and might even zigzag right into one of the other two.

So instead we asked, "How often do they eat?" He explained that a zebra will last the trio about three or four days. As we rode over the next hill, we found a zebra herd. We hoped that one would be missing tonight.

On the eve of the race, the runners were apprehensively talking about race day. Most of us had seen episodes of the *Wild Kingdom* and *National Geographic*. We nervously joked that predators go after the old, very young, solitary, and/or injured animals.

So, it was important not to be the slowest in the group, run alone, or limp!!! We identified the risk and had a plan. All of us managed to finish the race without any problems.

ANALYSIS PARALYSIS

"Analysis paralysis" can be a major problem with the planning process. This occurs when a person be-

comes so entangled in the planning that the plan never gets executed. This was my major problem.
I can always find something wrong or a good reason not to proceed. There were several reasons behind my "analysis paralysis."

1. **I knew too much**. - The more you know, the more reasons you can find for a plan to fail.
2. **I'm afraid of failure or risk-taking**. - Why should I risk moving outside of my comfort zone? After all, my comfort zone is nice and warm.
3. **I can't depend on other people**. - "They" are the reasons that projects fail and I don't control "them."

I could spend years developing the perfect plan and miss thousands of opportunities along the way. At some point, I had to accept the unknown problems, deal with the risks and execute the plan. I surrounded myself with reliable people and executed the plan.

We realized that we rarely had all of the information that was needed to completely develop and execute the plan. So, we actually built the task of "re-planning" into the project plan. In large projects, many decisions can't be made until the analysis is complete. This leaves many TBD (to be determined) tasks.

These tasks are documented and expounded throughout the project. Thus, the plan was a living organism which grew throughout the project.

"Analysis paralysis manifests itself through exceedingly long phases of project planning, requirements gathering, program design and modeling, with little or no extra value created by those steps."

Source: Wikipedia, the Free Encyclopedia

"If you don't have confidence, you'll always find a way not to win."

- Carl Lewis

Great Wall of China Marathon Sign

GAINING SUPPORT FROM YOUR RESOURCES

A resource is anything that you need to accomplish your goal. This includes people, money, and materials. When putting together your plan, it's always important to identify all of your resources.

A friend defined a resource as a

REliable **SOURCE**

An unreliable resource must be offset with one or more reliable backups. For example, your primary babysitter choice may be a "no cost" parent. However, if the parent is unreliable, a drop off daycare facility or alternate babysitter may be your back-ups. However, an additional resource (i.e. money) may be required.

People Resources

Many projects fail because the people resources weren't aware that they were a part of the project. This also implies that they were not involved in developing the plan.

Frequently, it's assumed that the resources are available or supportive while the plan is developed. How many times were you "volunteered" for a project and you were never asked about your current assignments? Or you were asked to support a project without having any input?

"A lack of planning on your part doesn't constitute an emergency on my part."

- Unknown

A fur seal on the course during the Antarctica Marathon.

You felt like your opinion was insignificant. Also, you either had to drop or delay an existing project or reassign it to someone else. You felt that you were constantly fighting fires and never saw a project through to completion.

To combat this problem, after you've completed your plan, you should print it out. Needless to say, this implies that the plan is in writing. It should include at a minimum:

- Tasks
- Durations
- Start Date
- End Date
- Predecessors
- Comments
- Resources (People, Money, and Materials)

It's important to review your plan with your resources prior to executing it. You'll need their approval. If this is a plan to achieve a personal goal, your resources may be surprised that you actually have a printed plan with their name on it. (Seeing their name on a plan is good for their ego.) For the most part, many people have never seen a printed, personal project plan.

As your resource reviews your plan, they'll probably offer tips and suggestions. They may be so impressed that you actually have a written plan that they'll provide more resources than you requested. They'll realize that you mean business and plan to succeed. Everyone wants to be a part of a winning team and consistent winners always have a plan.

MONTETARY RESOURCES

Most plans need money. It's not unusual for financial problems to occur during the project. Funds were redirected from my projects to more critical corporate problems. Once, I lost my tuition reimbursement benefits when I changed jobs and had to pay for my classes.

When creating the plan, identify all of your financial requirements. If it's to pursue a degree in the evening, your costs should not only include tuition, but books, dinner or snacks, additional gasoline, tutors, internet access, laptop, babysitters, and software.

Talk with other people who have accomplished the goal and learn about their expenses. As you review your plan with your resources, ask them about any expenses that you may have omitted. They may be so impressed with your plan that they may offer to fund the project. Also, as you developed your risk mitigation plan, you should include those costs into your budget.

Your back-up financial resources may be your savings accounts, loans against your 401K, credit card cash advances, bank or credit union loans, or monies from family members. In any case, it's important to identify these financial resources, and in some cases, get pre-approved before you begin your project. The time it takes to begin the process of obtaining financial resources "in the heat of the project battle" may spell defeat for your plan.

It's important to budget for a celebration or "thank you" event for your resources. It could be something a simple as a lunch, some flowers, or a thank you card. Or it could be as elaborate as a family cruise.

MATERIAL RESOURCES

Material resources are the things that you'll actually need to complete your plan. These could be anything from running shoes, jelly beans, and electrolytes for marathons, to study guides for certification exams.

PROJECT PLAN REVIEW PROCESS

Once the plan is completed, it must be reviewed by your resources and support team. Hopefully, at least one of them has previously achieved your goal. You may draw from their personal experience to provide additional advice. Also, consider looking for plans on the Internet.

Due to the length of most plans, schedule an initial meeting with the reviewer to go over the high points. Instruct them to focus on the missing tasks, dependencies, and resources. Ask them about any problems that they encountered while reaching the goal. Encourage them to be critical.

Let them know that you value their time and will schedule a follow-up meeting. This gives them a chance to contemplate their previous experiences and to enhance your plan. During the follow-up meeting, listen to their concerns, make the appropriate modifications, and thank them for their time.

Achievement Equation Component #4

EXECUTION

Execute

Definition: to produce in accordance with a plan or design; to perform or accomplish something, as an assigned task.

Source: *Dictionary.com*

Fin Del Mundo (Argentina) Marathon Medal

"A good plan, that's well executed, is better than an excellent plan on paper."

- General George S. Patton

Great Wall of China Marathon Sign

HOW EXECUTION BECAME A PART OF THE EQUATION

I went to the mailbox and retrieved the letter that I had been dreading. I had been placed on academic suspension. The better part of that winter break was spent blaming everyone for my personal failures.

- The teachers were too hard.
- They assigned too much homework.
- I came from a disadvantaged background.
- They didn't test me over the material that I knew.
- They didn't give me enough time to study.
- The textbooks were poorly written.
- The classes were too long.
- The professors talked too fast.
- The professors wrote too fast and erased the material before I could write it down.
- The classes were too early in the morning.
- The students weren't helpful and were snobby.
- The classes didn't relate to my major.
- My test grades didn't reflect my real knowledge of the subject matter.
- The professors didn't ask the right questions.
- Family problems had distracted me.

Over the next few months, I found plenty of people who supported my views. In other words, I had successfully developed a network of people who supported my failure. We had great "pity parties." They were actually happy to see me fail. My failure supported and further justified their failures. I had lived up to their low expectations of me. I blamed everyone, except me.

It wasn't my fault. It was The System. I was The Victim. I was not responsible for my failures.

I spent the better part of three or four months blaming The System. Then I realized that it was my fault. The System was not going to change. I had to accept responsibility for my actions before any progress could be made. I realized that I had spent too much time going to parties and spending time with friends. I was also procrastinating.

I had to learn to make the right decisions regarding how I spent my time. My college transcript didn't have a place for my excuses. It didn't have a place to list the parties that I had attended, the friends I had made, or my expertise at games. It only had room for the semester, course numbers, names, and grades. Not excuses.

I realized that I had to work hard to reach my goals. If everyone could get a college degree, the degree would have little or no value. I also realized that earning the degree was my first test at setting and reaching long-term goals.

In elementary, middle, and high school, the legal and academic institutions set my long-term goals. They "forced" me to go to school from kindergarten through the twelfth grade. If I didn't go to school, the authorities would contact my parents, search for me, and return me to classes. Education for people younger than 18 was not optional.

"Motivation is the link between goal setting, planning and execution."

- Tony Reed

A Humpback Whale in Antarctica.

However, after 18, education was optional. The colleges didn't force me to do anything. They didn't even call my parents when I failed. They didn't even call me. They didn't remind me about upcoming assignments or exams.

They provided long-term road maps (or plans) via the college catalog and the degree programs. The short-term road map was the course syllabus. I had to motivate myself to execute the plans and achieve the goals.

If I wanted a degree, I had to work for it. Earning a degree was my first test at goal setting, short- and long-term planning, self-motivating, and executing. This realization was a major turning point in my life.

If I wanted to succeed, it was up to me. I had to accept responsibility for my failures. I had to objectively determine the:

- reasons for my failures
- roles in my failures
- lessons learned from my mistakes
- plans for avoiding failures in the future

Just like my college transcript, there would be no place in my life to write my excuses. Successfully executing my life's plan was completely up to me.

EXECUTION & ITS RELATED OBSTACLES

The execution process is cyclical.

1. You focus on completing each individual task. If your plan is well defined, each task is small and manageable.
2. While executing the task, you motivate yourself and your resources. As you complete enough tasks, your resources will start motivating you to finish. They can smell a winner and they want to be a part of your winning team.
3. You look at your previously completed tasks to draw your strength, self trust, self confidence, and self motivation to complete your current and future tasks.

It's important that you monitor yourself throughout the process and take appropriate breaks. And of course, celebrate when you finish.

The more you accomplish; the more personal history you have to motivate you. When running through 2,400 feet of ankle deep mud during the Antarctica Marathon, I thought about the non-stop rains during the Hartford Marathon.

As I approached the foot of the Collins Glacier, I thought about the 3,600 steps of the Great Wall of China Marathon. As the winds gusted up to 40 MPH, thoughts about the long windy stretches during the Tri-Cities Marathon came to mind. The biting cold temperatures reminded me of playing on our high school's soccer team in the cold St. Louis winters.

The Achievement Equation: Your Formula For Success

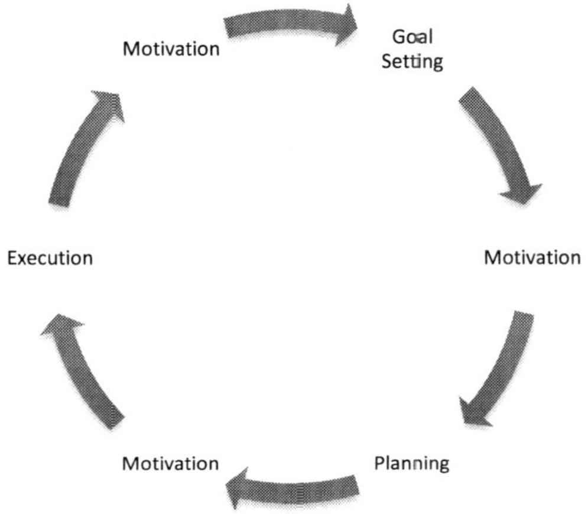

The view from the top of the Collins Glacier turna-round during the Antarctica Marathon.

There are several barriers that prevent people from executing their plan to achieve their goals. Some of these barriers include:

- Dealing with dead bodies and spider love
- Managing unplanned events and stress
- Procrastinating
- Delegating

DEAD BODIES & SPIDER LOVE

I was watching the late Tammy Faye Bakker Messner on VH1's The Surreal Life. She was telling an audience about her experiences with making difficult and personal life-changing decisions. She used an analogy of carrying a dead body on her back. The physical weight of the body slows you down.

As the body decomposes, you get the diseases and infections from the dead body. Ultimately, the dead body can kill you. You have to make a decision. You may carry the dead body and die. Or you may cut it loose and live. The choice is yours.

Several times in my life I had found myself carrying dead bodies. The dead body is symbolic. It can be an unsupportive person. It can be a bad habit, such as smoking, drug use, drinking, or lack of physical activity. It can also be a fear that prevents you from moving forward. Again, self examination or working with a professional, such as a physician, counselor, or therapist, will reveal the dead bodies and possible solutions for removing them.

PANIC ATTACK AT 35,000 FEET

A dead body almost stopped me from achieving my goal of running a marathon on all seven continents. In July, 2004, I headed to Europe. It was my first long plane trip. The plane wasn't full and I was able to occupy two seats. I combined the multi-country business trip with a side visit to Denmark for the marathon. Everything went smoothly.

A year later, I prepared to visit Australia to run a marathon on my birthday. Since I had to switch airline carriers, I had no control over the seating arrangements. Furthermore, the plane was packed with about 200 middle and high school students heading to Sydney for a music retreat.

I was assigned "the seat from hell," a window seat. I prefer isle seats due to my leg length. I can put one or both legs in the isle to stretch out. Now, I was shoved in a tight corner with no way to easily get out. When the person in front of me reclined their seat, it was about a foot from my face. I felt like I was in a sardine can. Minutes later, I felt a small panic attack approaching. As it turned out, tight spaces were my "dead body."

I left my seat and found a flight attendant. I pulled out my credit cards and asked to be moved to business class. It didn't matter how much it cost. Unfortunately, business class was full and he couldn't conduct the transaction anyway. I explained my problem and he offered some helpful tips to make the flight bearable.

"You cannot fix, what you cannot face."

- James Baldwin

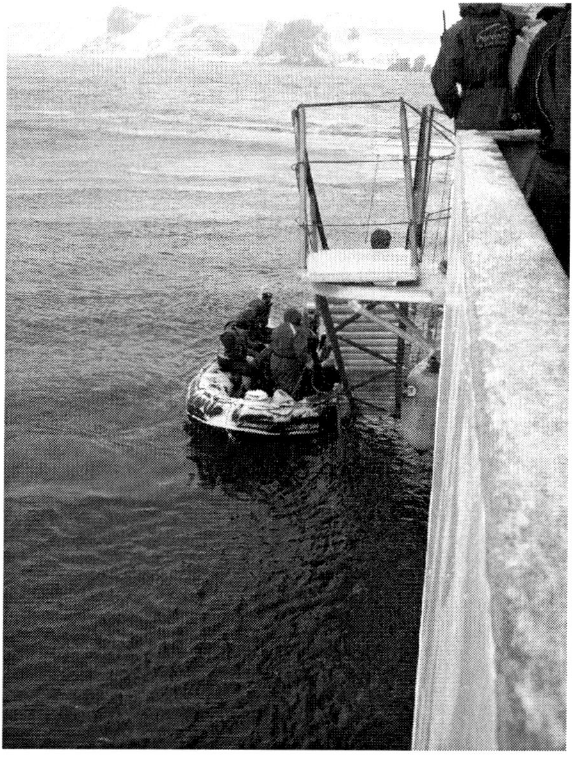

Zodiac boats transported us to the start of the Antarctica Marathon.

If I hadn't acknowledged and cut this dead body lose, I would not have flown to China, Antarctica, Argentina, and Kenya to complete my goal.

The dead body can also be a person, such as a relative, spouse, close friend, or co-worker. It's the person who offers you discouragement, however small. They may even discourage you "for your own good."

Since they don't want to see you fail, they'll discourage you taking a risk, moving outside of your comfort zone (or the comfort zone they've built for you), and exploring something new.

Unfortunately, some dead bodies are close family members. They'll try to use the relationship to satisfy their personal needs at your expense. After all, they're family. And family members don't turn their backs on each other. They're supposed to support each other, regardless of the circumstances. This is a "guilt trip." Your hard earned money was their money. And their money was their money.

A morning talk show host described this situation as "spider love." If you ask a spider, "Who do you love?" Their response is, "The fly." He catches the fly in his web and wraps it up in the web. When he's hungry, he sucks the juice out of the fly. The spider truly loves the fly. He sucks the life right out of it.

You have to recognize the spiders and dead bodies in your life and determine how to deal with them before you can successfully execute your plan.

STRESS MODEL

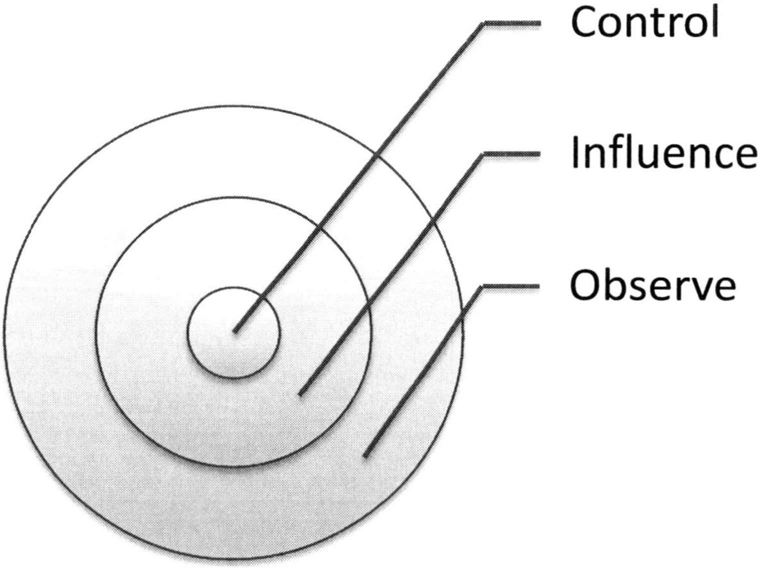

I realized that people wanted me to sacrifice my dreams and hard earned accomplishments for their irresponsible behavior and small comfort zones. I made a conscious decision to keep those close relatives and other individuals at a distance.

I had to cut the rope, drop the dead bodies, and kill the spiders for my personal sanity and success.

MANAGING UNPLANNED EVENTS & STRESS

When a crisis arises, such as an unplanned event, immediately classify it into one of three categories:

1. **Observe** – This is an event that you have absolutely no control over. Therefore, don't stress out over it. You must accept it and plan for it.
2. **Influence** – If you can influence the outcome of an event to your advantage, then try to do that. Keep in mind that someone else has control over the event. Thus, you should not be stressed over their decision. It's their right to control the outcome.
3. **Control** – This is an event that you can control. Since you have control, you should not stress out over your decision. You decide what's in your best interest and take the appropriate action.

Another way to look at these three areas is to compare them with children. You can control a baby. When the child starts school, you can influence their behavior. When they graduate from high school, you can only observe them!!!

"We kill time, time buries us."

– Joaquim Marchado de Assis

An avalanche in Antarctica.

FIN DEL MUNDO WHITE OUT

On the eve of Argentina's Fin Del Mundo Marathon, we were looking down at the beautiful city of Ushuaia. In less than a minute, the snow was falling so fast, that the visibility was reduced to less than 50 yards.

About 15 minutes later, the snow stopped. Throughout the day we saw the weather change from perfect running temperatures to blinding snowstorms in a matter of minutes.

We couldn't control or influence the weather. The only thing that we could control was the clothing we wore. Thus, we didn't worry about the weather. Instead, we focused on our clothes.

We finally decided to dress in layers. Instead of wearing a single layer of heavy, winter clothes, we would wear multiple layers of light shirts, pants, and jackets. If the weather warmed up, we could easily remove the outer layers of clothes, tie them around our waist, and remain cool. This pre-planning allowed us to finish the marathon with minimal stress.

PROCRASTINATION

Procrastination is a major problem for me. It's my drug and I'm a recovering addict. Once an addict, always an addict. It's easy to slip back into this problem if you aren't aware of your actions—or should I say, lack of actions. Thus, I constantly fight not to procrastinate. I realized that by developing a good project plan, task list, or to do list, I decrease the probability

The view of Ushuaia, Argentina from my hotel.

The same view 15 minutes later.

of procrastination. I hold myself accountable for making the deadline. I try to:

1. **Break up the work** into small chucks.
2. **Commit to a specific start date**. This should not be January 1st. Too many people start life changing events on this same stress-filled date. If something is important enough to begin on January 1st, then it's important enough to begin today.
3. **Identify a specific end date**. If the task doesn't have an end date, it doesn't have to be finished!!!
4. **Think about the final celebration and reward**.
5. **Consider the number of people that you'll let down**, such as your resources, if you're late.

Also, I take advantage of PC-based tools, such as MS Outlook, to set up reminders and alerts about upcoming events and tasks.

DELEGATING

Nobody can do it better than you can. You know how to do it your way. You can do it the right way. You do it yourself.

I was responsible for a highly visible major software implementation project. If we failed, we expected to hear about it in the U.S. Congress and read about it in the news media. Failure may have led to the agency's closure.

"It is not the light that is needed, but the fire."

– Fredrick Douglas

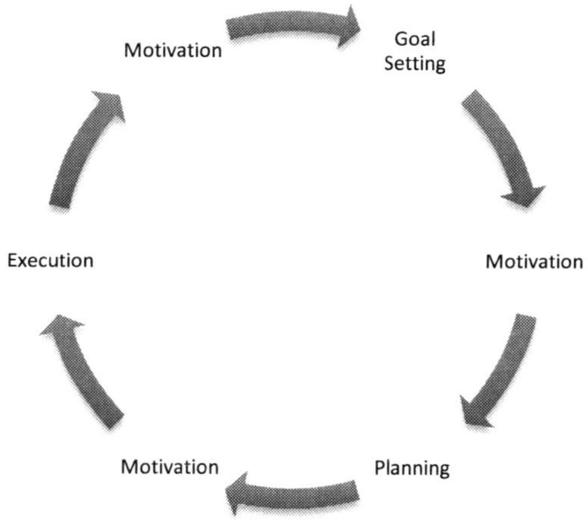

I worked with my project team to develop a detailed project plan. After we identified the tasks, dependencies, durations, and dates, we assigned resources to the tasks. Due to its importance, I was involved in many tasks. The plan was complete.

Later that day, I discovered a new report in the project planning software. It was a "resource leveling" report. It indicated that I was way overcommitted on the project. Based on my assigned tasks, I needed to work several hundred hours a week or learn to trust my staff and to delegate.

The Achievement Equation

AE

=

G x M x P x E

Where values G, M, P, and E are binary

THE ACHIEVEMENT EQUATION'S SUCCESS FORMULA

The Achievement Equation's (AE) components are

Goal setting (G)
Motivating (M)
Planning (P)
Executing (E)

Without a SMART goal, you can't develop and execute a plan. An unclear goal yields an equally unclear result. A goal setter without motivation and a plan is like a dreamer who stays in bed.

Motivation is the string that connects the SMART goal, the plan, and the execution. Without motivation, the plan may never be developed or executed.

A highly motivated person without a plan is like a dog chasing his tail. There's just a lot of dust from where the dog was running. There's a lot of action, but no results.

Let's assume that each component is represented by a binary value. That's to say, each component's value is either zero or one.

The Achievement Equation becomes

$$A = G \times M \times P \times E = (\text{Zero or One})$$

This is a multiplicative equation. Any number multiplied by zero yields zero. In our equation,

- You either set a SMART goal (value = 1) or don't (value = 0).
- You're either highly motivated to reach your SMART goal (value = 1) or not (value = 0).
- You either highly motivated to develop a good plan to reach your SMART goal (value = 1) or you try to wing it (value = 0).
- You're either highly motivated to execute the plan to reach your SMART goal (value = 1) or you do nothing (value = 0).

Since the equation is

$$AE = G \times M \times P \times E = (\text{Zero or One})$$

AE always equals one or zero. Thus, if you fail to follow through on any one of the components, AE equals zero. In other words, you achieve nothing.

All of us know successful people who achieved goals without fully implementing all of these components. They had luck. The equation may be modified to allow for luck (assigned value = L). Luck is also binary. The equation now becomes

$$AE = (G \times M \times P \times E) - L = (\text{Zero or One})$$

Now, any or all of the values for G, M, P, and E may be zero. If luck is available (value = 1), then the goal is achieved. The problem with luck, such as winning the lottery, is that you can't control it or predict when it will occur.

The Achievement Equation

AE

=

G x M x P x E

Where values G, M, P, and E are binary

WHAT'S NEXT?

For as long as I've been setting and achieving goals, people tend to ask me one question, "What's next?" Whether I'm travelling internationally or taking a training run around Dallas' White Rock Lake, any conversation with a marathoner leads to same question, "What's next?"

Over the years, I began to notice four interesting reactions or by-products to achieving goals.

First, people live vicariously through the accomplishments of achievers. They want to say that they personally know someone who has achieved an individual goal. It could be completing a triathlon, bicycling across the U.S., competing in an open water swimming competition, or earning an undergraduate degree in your forties. You become the person that your friends will talk about at happy hours, the water cooler, and at church. You made it!!!

"I always had some-thing to shoot for each year: to jump one inch farther."

\- Jackie Joyner-Kersee

Humpback Whale in Antarctica

Second, people expect you to continue to set and achieve goals. They don't expect failure. They expect you to succeed. They'll want to be able to continue telling their friends about your adventures and accomplishments. They become your cheerleaders and supporters. Everyone wants to support a winner. And you're a winner that they can bank on.

During the Great Wall of China Marathon tour, several of the runners bonded together. One evening at dinner, we began discussing what we would do after we finished marathons on all seven continents.

For the first time, I began to realize that life without a goal was dull and unexciting. It was actually depressing to think about life after running marathons on the seven continents. Since I was the computer geek and brought my laptop on the trip, I was given the task of finding the Seven Wonders of the World on the Internet. Yes, we were contemplating running marathons in or near the locations of the Wonders.

Much to our surprise, there were many different "seven wonders" to choose from, such as:

- Ancient Wonders
- Modern Wonders
- Underwater Wonders
- Architectural Wonders
- Man-Made Wonders

We even talked about running marathons on the seven continents again, but running them on islands. This might take us to:

- Jamaica (North America)
- New Zealand (Oceania)
- Japan (Asia)
- King George Island (Antarctica)
- Madagascar (Africa)
- Galapagos Islands (South America)
- Iceland (Europe)

We realized that no matter what goal we set our eyes on, it would be exciting and fun.

The third thing about achieving goals relates to heroes. During a training run, I was joined by a stranger. He looked to be in his sixties. As it turned out, he was from my hometown of St. Louis. Instinctively, I asked him about the baseball Cardinals season.

He told me that he used to follow baseball religiously. Several years ago, he suffered a heart attack and had a triple bypass. While he was recovering, he decided to change his lifestyle. He got his doctor's approval and began running. Now, whenever he wants to see an athlete, he just looks in the mirror. He became his own hero.

After our conversation, I began noticing something about distance runners. Instead of wearing the jerseys of professional athletes, we wear our race t-shirts. Perhaps it's our way of saying that we're our own heroes and athletes.

As you set and achieve goals, don't be surprised if you become less interested in the lives of entertainers and athletes and more focused on your own goals.

The last observation about achievers is that they become the best cheerleaders. They've "been through the fire" and "crossed the burning sands." They know what it's like to have to dig deep when you feel that no one else is around to help you.

For these reasons, achievers tend to motivate and inspire others in reaching their goals. In turn, these people may help you in your future endeavors or adventures.

The Great Wall of China Marathon Medal

GOMOPLEX™ is a life-style supplement. It's taken men-tally. After years of research, it was determined that by combining four previously separate elements into one supplement, a synergic effect occurs. People have been known to achieve their personal and professional goals. **GOMOPLEX™** is based on the Achievement Equation.

POSSIBLE SIDE EFFECTS OF GOMOPLEX™ include a sense of accomplishment, personal and professional fulfillment, excitement, happiness, priceless moments, and high levels self confidence. These side effects are contagious and may spread to friends and relatives.

GOMOPLEX™ users have been known to break sales records, complete projects on time, within budget, and to specifications, improve productivity, graduate from school, run marathons around the world, and finish triathlons.

WARNINGS: GOMOPLEX™ should not be taken by people who want to lead dull and directionless lives. It should not be taken by people who want to be lazy or inactive. People, who don't want to achieve goals, should not take **GOMOPLEX™**. They may find that they'll exceed their personal expectations, overcome their fears, and accomplish something spectacular.

GOMOPLEX™ has been approved by the FDA (Fun and Daring Administration).